YOU
CAN
LOOK
UP

YOU CAN LOOK UP

ARLENE FIFER-DEAN

TATE PUBLISHING
AND **ENTERPRISES, LLC**

Published by Tate Publishing & Enterprises, LLC
127 E. Trade Center Terrace | Mustang, Oklahoma 73064 USA
1.888.361.9473 | www.tatepublishing.com

Tate Publishing is committed to excellence in the publishing industry. The company reflects the philosophy established by the founders, based on Psalm 68:11,
"The Lord gave the word and great was the company of those who published it."

Book design copyright © 2014 by Tate Publishing, LLC. All rights reserved.
Cover design by Joel Uber
Interior design by Mary Jean Archival

Published in the United States of America

ISBN: 978-1-62994-449-4
1. Poetry / Subjects & Themes / Inspirational & Religious
2. Poetry / General
14.01.03

Dedication

I dedicate this book to my husband, who knows that you can always look up. I am also dedicating this book to my friends and family, who need to know that they can look up. I am also dedicating this book to Liberty Christian Center and the Vessels of Faith bible study for teaching people how to look up.

Contents

Foreword

When I first met Arlene, we instantly became friends. I never thought our friendship would last this long. When things are going wrong, she always calls me to ask what is wrong. Although sometimes it is hard for her to speak the words, she has learned to put words into poems. Her first book titled *Do Not Give Up* helped me to smile when I felt like giving up on my family and myself. I felt I wasn't productive in my life. She was there through every surgery I have had, and for me and my husband, she always has words of wisdom. I want her to know the poem titled *Another Chance* has helped me to look at things in a different way. We sometimes forget that God gave us another chance, so we must learn to give people another chance. The poem "Along the Way" helps me to smile because she is right. Sometimes you don't want to smile, but the best way to get through a problem is to see how long you can keep that smile. She is a precious friend, and I am very proud that God has put her in my life. With this second book, I know she will continue to put her wisdom into poems, and they will help someone like they have helped me.

Your special friend,
Trena Hope

A Church

It is time for the church to arise
To show effort and not just surmise
Begin your journey and find your task
Do not just dream in the bask

Learn how to live with might
Let go of anger, also spite
An atmosphere of truth and glory
Work with God to not worry

Start your day by being bright
Try not to leave and be in a flight
Whether you are happy or sad
Try not to let things make you mad

Pray often and give God praise
Adhere to church and its ways
Give Jesus a thank-you for what he did
Let your heart open and sense the valid

The church holds the warriors, the body of Christ
Made of people going to the tryst
The foundation and building joined together
But not making it become a tether

When you are planted in church to play the role
Do not fall apart, become whole
Grow and be strong with another
Do not walk away from each other

A Sign

When the lights go out
And you feel the doubt
God says, "Place your hand on mine
I will give you a sign"

He says, "Let me love you
Be there for you"
It will be all right
Whether it be day or night

I want you near
I don't want you to fear me
God says, "Just place your hand on mine
Let me give you a sign"

He says, "I will let you love me
Be there with me"
And I know it's right
The dark does have light

With every passing day
We will learn what to say
God will be there too
A sign is waiting for you

Almost Time

The day will come
And angels will hum
The day will be bright
There will be so much light

At that time we will see
What is to come and what is to be
Days and nights also will be
The way that they should be

No more darkness
No more pain for us
Good shall enter where problems were
God will be with us for sure

It is almost time
For all the words to rhyme
Everything will come around
To the highest mound

It is needed, it will be
Hang on tight, you will see
Stay with the plan, do not grieve
Many beautiful things we will receive

God shows us where to go
He knows our patience has to show
It is almost time for the good
It is almost in the right mood

Beauty

Such beauty is everywhere
Here, there, and anywhere
Look for it as you look around
In front of you, or on a mound

Sometimes right in front of us
Look for positive, look for plus
Negative is not to be
Good and right for you and me

Hold your head up high
Whether morning or night
Beauty is all around
It is captured with the sound

So you see, good will be
The promise is to you and me
See it now, it will blend
With God, all will fall into place and mend

Be Aware

Always take time to be aware
Take time to notice, time to care
Know what is going on around you
Find out what is right and what is true

If you know how things need to be
Something out of place won't be hard to see
It is important to be organized
Then your way of life is memorized

Evil plays games, good plays right
You need to know day from night
Be able to figure out the truth
And it always helps when you have proof

In all you do, take care
In your life, become aware
Step forward without suspension
Do not have apprehension

Become Free

One day you notice what you give
Like granules going through a sieve
Filtering out the good and bad
Then you know you are no longer sad

Always pray throughout the day
Always have something nice to say
Become the person you want to be
Love yourself and be free

Do your best not to be melancholy
Read your Bible, it can be a monopoly
Lift your spirits up high
Enjoy your life, do not cry

Be assertive to what is not resolved
Let worries go to be absolved
Care about the ones you love
Also love God up above

Begin to Change

It is the beginning of a new tier
Changes will be made from what you hear
Live your life as you have never lived
Begin to organize each and every grid

Solemnly filtering through the light
Take the chance and hold on tight
Be aware of how you react
Here is now, and this is that

Adhere to what you are doing
It is no one you will be fooling
Get it right, don't lose sight
This will be a good flight

Take your knowledge and use it now
Don't wonder if you know how
All that matters will apply
Spread your wings and learn to fly

Be His Children

As we come closer to God
We look up to him and nod
To do what we should
Before not knowing that we could

Everyone around you is there at his feet
They will fall to their knees and not be discreet
They will feel the love, the peace, the grace
The calmness will show in their face

A relationship now understood
With a destiny that is good
Holding on and giving praise
At times to him even our arms will raise

We are his children, he is our Father
He wants us bright and not somber
He allows us to make a choice
If we want, we can hear his voice

Look ahead and see what lies before you
Look ahead and see God's plan for you
Look ahead and be not afraid
Look ahead and see what has been made

Be Humble

Be ever so humble, my child
It is you that I love, even when wild
You know your destiny in this world
You know where you belong, become unfurled

You are mine, and I love you
Open up and remember my gift to you
See the beauty once again
Never lose sight of it and always win

The time to rejoice is here
You are ready, you are there
Love is everywhere upon you
Love is everywhere, and I love you

Do not give up on me
Do not forsake me
Love me as I love you
Be proud in whatever you do

You will live strong and meek
You will never again be weak
So come to me with arms opened wide
Stand by me, and be by my side

Be not afraid my child
Be powerful, yet be mild
Soon you will see my gift to you
And your gift to me is to know I love you

Happiness is the very key
I love you, you love me
Close your eyes, kneel, and pray
Come back to me this very day

Bless This House

Bless this house, oh Lord, I pray
Make it safe night and day
Allow us to be there when needed
Remember it has now been seeded

We believe you and love you
We will succumb to you
Where we should be
Allow us to see

Now and then hold us close
We all need a good dose
Allow us to show
We are going to grow

When we do not know what to do
We will always come to you
This is not fake, but real
We are learning as we feel

Come to Me

He says, "Come to me today"
I ask this in every way
Be ready, prepared, and acknowledged
Ever so engulfed and loved

Ready to reap the harvest you sow
Willing to be responsible and know
Today is your beginning and start
Be ready and be pure in heart

A beautiful church surrounded by angels
And a bell that dangles
To know at any time you can come
You are accepted, you are not overcome

Do not be overcome with fear, anger, or worry
Coming to God, you will never be sorry
Remember what you have learned
A time when so much you yearned

You did not give up, you stayed
With you I always prayed
Now you can follow through
Do what you are supposed to do

Dance with Me

This poem is dedicated to my husband.

Dance with me for the rest of my life
I want to be yours, I am your wife
Love me as you have loved no other
I don't want to be with another

I want to hold you, feel you, have you close
Bloom together beautiful as a rose
Be there when I need you, me there for you
Try to be sincere in whatever we do

God, be with us, teach us right
I need to know we will be all right
Watch over us, guide, and bless
So we understand and not have to guess

So dance with me, vibrations in tune
I need your touch always, I am not immune
Hear the music, feel the peace within
Dance with me and give in

Do Not Give Up on God

Humbly before you we kneel, Father
Asking all people around us to gather
Together we fall and pray
Asking for you to show us your way

It is within your realm
To stand before us at the helm
Lead us and show us what to do
It cannot be done without you

We love and need you, Father
Above you there is no other
We are willing to prove we want to grow
Help us and show us what we need to know

We cry out for your attention
We are all your humble children
Praying for help is not odd
Do not give up on God

Do Not Run From God

Do not let the problem control you
Do not let evil overtake you
Do not let it force you to run and hide
Do not forget God, do abide

Do control the problem
Do know the good emblem
Do stop, be seen, and find a solution
Do remember God and our dimension

In Jesus's name you are protected
The bad around you is detected
You have the strength to give it to God
Do not run from God

Dreams

Dreams that can rule and overtake you
So real, so strong, so true
Where will they lead you next
Will you recognize the text

When you close your eyes to rest
Wonder if you are going through a test
So clear and vivid in your mind
You wonder what you are going to find

Some are familiar, some from your past
Others are unclear and slip in fast
Dreams can seem real and be a task
Maybe just a fantasy you mask

Ask God to help you
He will hear you
He will catch you in time
Support and help you climb

Everything

Between you and me
Everything God can see
He knows your heart
So do your part

Let no one deceive you
Let no one abuse you
Look to God for protection
Turning to him is the right direction

Enjoy your life and learn to live
Savor a moment, the times you give
Be ever respondent to the ones you love
Have trust and faith in God above

Be not ashamed of what you have done
You are not the only one
Sometimes life can confuse you
Make it clear God can use you

Accept God as your savior
Give him praise and favor
Allow his love to embrace you
He is always there for you

Falling Leaves

Falling leaves are all around
It is very still with no sound
The day will come for us to see
What will come and what will be

The seasons change
Our lives we rearrange
When it is very still
We can see God's will

The leaves we rake and gather
But does it really matter
As they fall to the ground
People will fall and hear no sound

The time is now, we shall not fall
It is now time, it is our call
It is very still with no sound
The falling leaves do surround

We pick them up as they fall
We cannot lose them, so pick up all
Gather the leaves, it is the season
Yet do we really know the reason

Find the Mask

In the midst of what we see
Is where the truth lies, it will begin to be
Look slowly and take your time
Then make sure every sentence will rhyme

Be careful as you hear the sounds
Still keep going over the mounds
Now your pain has been cleared
You understand what you once feared

Forsake all others, hear their plea
Help when needed, do not flee
Time is important for everyone around
Take the time to look and hear the sound

Be ever grateful for what has been given you
Live, learn, love, and be you
Many masks around you see
You see the truth, you see me

The Lord is willing, always there for you to ask
You have to see the person wearing the mask
Sort out to find the one in need
Help someone and take the lead

Friends

This poem is dedicated to my friend Cathie for over forty-five years.

Friends like sisters
Everlasting like whispers
Holding the memories close and near
Wondering what next will happen here

If knowing what next will be
Time gone past, like a flowing sea
Feeling good and bad from days gone by
Seeing truth of each other with a sigh

Through the years keeping in touch
Sometimes it was needed much
Then again at times just a little
Trying to work it out like a riddle

Friends like sisters are
Sometimes close, sometimes far
At times they will fight
But agree at times they might

They struggle to find hopes and dreams
Putting it together, like sewing seams
Finding comfort in being there
One for another, the lives they share

God and Jesus Do Not Lie

Our lives go through many paths
There are good, sad, and sometimes wraths
We learn, we try, in the end we die
But God and Jesus do not lie

We try to do it right
If we are wise, we might
There are so many walls to climb
We get tired, we are sublime

If we falter, whom to blame
Ourselves, people around us, or just shame
If we make it to the other side
Did we make it, or was it just one ride

Always look for what is bright
Always try to face your fight
God and Jesus do not lie
Always give it one more try

God Is with Us

We will understand and see
The truth is to be
Stand by us he will
He is with us, it is his will

God is with us, we are his
We are important, we are his
Every one of us will know what to do
It will be shown, so it is true

The dark has now been lifted
It is gone, so it is lifted
The work will now begin
The beauty will now be in

It is time to rejoice
It is time to hear his voice
No longer will we be sad
No longer will he be mad

Let us sing and have grace
It is time to give great praise
Rejoice, I say, be happy this day
People are coming this way

God and Jesus do not lie
It is now time to try
Feel the peace within
Look up to God, Jesus will win

God knows what you need
God knows what to heed
Hang on ever so tightly
Never letting go, not even lightly

Make it through the problem
You can do it, so be the emblem
Become a leader and help find
The happiness for all mankind

Sooner or later, there is always change
There is always something to rearrange
Do not worry, you will be all right
Through every day and every night

God is with you every day
He knows what you feel and want to say
Let him be your strength
Let him be with you through the length

Great Are You

God, you get our attention
Then give us protection
You teach us with your word
Great are you, Lord

You prepare us for battle
So we can hear every rattle
Balance us as we move forward
Great are you, Lord

You show us how to plant
What is needed and do not rant
Then next comes the harvest
You seem very modest

As time grows near
We have no fear
This is a temporary dwelling
We should not be rebelling

The day will come with joy sincere
When you come to us here
We will not need to hoard
Great are you, Lord

Harvest

Seeds planted earlier now begin to grow
Needing water so that they may sow
As flowers grow up a trellis for sun
It takes a while for beauty to be done

We need the seed of God's word
Plant seeds of faith to grow forward
It takes time for God's work to be done
To see the outcome of someone

Inspired by water and by us
Flowers and crops grow glorious
They will flourish and be bright
Striving for nurturing and light

As we get closer to God, we are zealous
Filled with the Holy Spirit within us
Devoted and obeying we begin to shine
Being loved we will not decline

Later for crops they begin the harvest
Ripened, mature, and being the best
Done for the season being gathered
A time for joy and know it mattered

As God is in control of our harvest
As his warriors, we are the best
He will bring us to our completion
There will be no deletion

Help Me, God

Help me to get through
Help me to be there for you

Help me, God, do not leave me alone
I need you by my side to condone

Like a scared child wanting to hide
Stay close to me by my side
I love you, God, and need you
Help me be strong to be strong with you

We cannot be like a child anymore
We have grown up and need God more
We need help to face our fears
To follow through as if using spears

We make our own decisions
We choose to see our visions
Whether life is good or bad
Life can make us happy or sad

Our fears will hold us back
The strength to overcome is what we lack
Look up to God and ask for help
Upon the mountain on the Alp

Humbly Before You

Father, we come humbly before you
We ask forgiveness from you
For our sins in this world
Like strong winds, they have hurled

We need you to help us be
Having strength to overcome and see
The beauty of what shall unfold
Not in hiding but out and bold

As we all come together and pray
We thank you on this very day
Joy with beauty everywhere
As we look on and stare

We are growing, and seeds are sowing
Ever there, ever knowing
The doors are open and wide
Feel free to see inside

Something beautiful is in the making
It is about to happen as we give, not taking
Be with us on this joyful day
We have obeyed, listened, you showed us the way

I Give It All to You

You give to me and call me
I will always be
Come and teach me how
To do it right now

I capture your presence
I love you, Lord, and sense
Your love for us, I pray
Take us and mold us today

Keep me where I need to be
Make sure your path I see
I come to you, I come to see
I want to always be

I give it all to you
I know I need you
Come to show us what to do
We very much need you

In Your Presence

Here in your presence
We become very tense
You grant us security
We become an obscurity

You teach us, and we honor you
We praise and worship like we need to
A feeling of warmth and energy
A feeling of peace and maturity

You fill us with your Holy Spirit
You release the greatness with merit
Accepted and wanted, we are
Whether we are close or far

Here in your presence, the beauty we feel
It is not obsolete, we know it is real
We give ourselves to you
Our lives have been made true

It Is Coming

Something beautiful
Something graceful
It is coming
It is coming

The Lord, our god, says so
He does not lie, he might get slow
A sense of humor, this we know
As we learn, we also grow

A time to smile
We have gone our mile
A church, there will be
For people all around with you and me

Peaceful, ever joyful
And ever so beautiful
And angels all around
Walking on the ground

Uplifting and never leaving
As you wonder if you are dreaming
It is coming
It is coming

It Will Be All Right

When there is nothing that can be done
When the time has been won
No matter what you do
It will follow through

It is not your choice to get it right
If not your responsibility to fight
Calm down, pray, and live
Just remember you help and give

It will be all right
God sees it through with the light
You cannot change what is meant to be
You cannot feel guilty for what you see

Understand the freedom has been granted
You cannot help if it is not wanted
Whether animal, person, or even a thing
If rejected, nothing helps, not even a sling

When God had to see his son upon a cross
He only could forsake his loss
The pain, the sadness, yet also the grace
He knew again he would see his face

Just Look Up

If the time is soon
And you feel immune
Remember that all is not lost
The wrong will pay the cost

Whenever something seems hard to reach
There is always a way to impeach
Life is too short to feel lost
Find your way and be the host

Let go of fear, look up
Begin to water your crop
Seeds will grow, and so will you
Listen to God, he will carry you

Do not feel lost, find your way
Look up to him every day
Look ahead and look up at the sky
Then you will soon understand why

Face your fears immediately
Tell the enemy to flee
Do not find yourself with arrears
Do not find yourself in tears

Keeping Distance Between

Loving you, needing you, only not able to
Instead keeping distance between God and you
They say you cannot make someone love God
But you can decide to lead them to God

Keeping the distance between
We already know what that will mean
Trying to struggle to hold on or let go
Making a difference above or below

For each other I hope we are always there
No matter what we will always care
I love you, God, you love me
That is still the way it will always be

Lay Down Your Burdens

Now is the time to lay down your burdens
Now is the time to let go of the ruins
Whether you are young or old
Whether you have silver or gold

You need to understand
Be worthy of this land
As sand trickles through your fingers
Remnants from life always lingers

Look upon the sun, the sky
See the beauty, it does not lie
Lay down your burdens now
The Lord, your god, will endow

We are here to live and learn
At times our hearts will yearn
We are here to learn how to live
Learn the way we are to give

The Lord is our teacher
As we lay down burdens ever
The time is now for you
Be ready to follow through

Life Can Be Good

You can always say life could be better
Always a reason why life would be better
Try saying life will be better
Do something to make it better

We have a choice to pick the way we live
Maybe we take from people, or we give
Your life has the chance to make amends
Put your life in God's hands

At times the way gets rough
Remain strong and be tough
You are responsible for you
You may decide what to do

Do not take in stride what is right
Make sure the end of the tunnel has light
You need to be positive about your life
Do not be negative and have strife

God will lead you and be by your side
He will lead the way along the ride
Do look up and lift your head high
Always make an effort to try

You need to be able to ask for help
Be sure you want it as some want help
Be able to receive what you asked for
And accept god as your savior

Life Is Precious

Life is too precious to waste
Too precious to live in haste
Feeling sorry for yourself
You actually put your life on a shelf

If you stop living
If you stop giving
You begin to unravel
You put down the gavel

Life has a meaning, a purpose for us
Instead of a minus, make it a plus
Remember our Father, which art in heaven
Remember the strength you have been given

Don't let life take you down
Go upward, go forward, wear your crown
Take that chance to live again
Remember what you believe in

Life takes love to survive
With that you can stay alive
Hallowed be thy name
With him your life will never be the same

Life is too precious to take away
Pray, follow, and find good in the day
Don't stop living
Don't stop giving

Look Up

In troubled times
When nothing rhymes
Keep your head high
Morning or night

Not giving up on what you must do
Do not give up on following through
The Lord knows your pain
The Lord knows your gain

If in shame, stop, look up
If in doubt, stop, look up
He is there, he is with you
He does care, he also needs you

Remember what you have been taught
You must be strong, you aught
Let God be your guide
Let God be by your side

He will not let you down
Do not make a frown
Stand, look up, and pray
There is coming a brighter day

Make It Through

Whenever times are tough
When everything seems too tough
Jump right in and take control
You can handle it, be on a roll

Take the time to see it through
It can make a difference for you
Learn to evaluate the situation
It will lead you to the solution

Arise and make it through
Be confident, be true
Be positive in what you do
Look for good in what you brew

Remember you are in God's hands
He has plans
Whatever you do
Make it through

My Child

Be ever so humble, my child
It is you that I love, even when wild
You know your destiny in this world
You belong, become unfurled

You are mine, and I love you
Open up and remember my gift to you
See the beauty once again
Never lose sight of it and always win

The time to rejoice is here
You are ready, you are there
Love is everywhere upon you
Love is everywhere, and I love you

Do not give up on me
Do not forsake me
Love me as I love you
Be proud in whatever you do

You will live strong and meek
You will never again be weak
Come to me with arms opened wide
Stand by me, and be by my side

Be not afraid, my child
Be powerful, yet be mild
Soon you will see my gift to you
Your gift to me is to know I love you

Happiness is the very key
I love you, you love me
Close your eyes, kneel, and pray
Come back to me this very day

Open the Doors

Tell us where to go now, Lord
Tell us as you read from a board
Show us what we need to do
Help us go and get through

Open the windows, unlock the doors
Give us the key to unlock yours
As we enter, let us in
Show us how the days have been

Give your permission to know it's true
The door will open to see you
Opening what was locked
It is no longer to be mocked

Being accepted means a lot
Not locked out, truth we have got
Feeling like we now belong
It is right, never wrong

Invite us in, be sincere
Know we should be here
The doors are open now
And to you we bow

Pastors

Pastors trying to follow through
With a vision they have to do
Build a church for people to pray
Do not give up, even on a bad day

The land is there
With weeds everywhere
The funds are low
Not many people we know

But the pastors are not lost
They will make it, whatever the cost
They need to know we will follow them
With God we will win, as he is the stem

Try to learn as much as you can
Even if before you ran
Show your church and pastor
You are getting stronger and show valor

The pastors always teach God's word
They never deceive or make things blurred
Keep on growing for all to win
God will follow then begin

Pay Attention

Pay attention and look around
See who needs prayed around
You can see it in their eyes
Or hear it in their cries

Know the meanings, truth or lies
Come between it, use the ties
Be prepared and know the way
You will know what to say

Be there when needed
It has been seeded
The time is right around the corner
You are not to be a mourner

Everything will be in place
Take the time to run the race
Take it slow
Then go

Prepare

I need to prepare for what lies ahead
I need to be ready for what is said
Not knowing the outcome, I pray
To make it safe and good, I say

For what must be
I must be ready
Change is allowed, let it be good
Bring positive to the mood

I sense a happening soon
It must follow the tune
Be close to us, God, as you pull us through
I know you help in what you do

Make us stronger for sure
Know what we ask is pure
Prepare us for the outcome
As we hear the rolling of the drum

Protection

Protect this church, oh Lord, I pray
Make it safe today and every day
We need your power and your grace
We need protection upon this place

Father, Son, and Holy Spirit
Bind to this with much merit
Protection we need for us all
This church cannot fall

Help it grow and multiply
Make it strong and many ply
As we build, let us feel the strength
Let it become in great length

We ask this in Jesus's name
Where is wild, now be tame
Let it all balance then
In Jesus's name, amen

Protect the Church

In all aspects, protect the church
Don't sit high upon a perch
There are angels all around
Listen carefully to the sound

Keep peace upon the people
Remember the reason for the steeple
Protect our worshippers as they pray
Protect the church in every way

Now is the time to ward off deception
That is surely the right selection
The enemy will try to bring us down
God will protect us so we won't drown

Protect the church wherever you are
Give it blessing like you wish on a star
Take care of matters within
Ever so strongly now begin

Your armor needs to be put on
Always ready night or dawn
Protect the church and watch your back
Work it out to the right track

Reaching Out

Be aware of what goes on around you
You need to notice everything you do
Focus not on one thing only
That can become very lonely

Reach out to our Heavenly Father
Do not think with you he will not bother
We need him as he needs us
For the glory, the outcome, the plus

Help each other and look around
Even when it's quiet, hear the sound
Instead of hurting, whining, or crying
Begin your life and start trying

Evaluate the way you live
Search out to whom you give
Make a change to do it right
Be ready for help day or night

It is amazing what is really here
Things you never saw but always near
You can always find good in something bad
Think of happy things when you are mad

Look in the mirror long enough
See yourself for real even if it is tough
We are loved and not forgotten
God lets us know we are loved often

Isaiah 45:10 NIV
"Woe to the one who says to a father
'What have you begotten'"

Somehow

My dear child
Calm your anger and be mild
You need to stop the mad
Somehow smile and be glad

It hurts God to see you cry
I tell the truth, not a lie
Somehow you need to believe
Find a way to retrieve

Love is for you and all around
Calm the outrage, hear the inner sound
Take the first step and go forward
Somehow keep your armor and sword

Life is a lesson, start to learn
Begin to grow and begin to earn
Somehow do more than listen
See all the good, see it glisten

Times get rough
Getting through is not enough
Move on to a higher level
Somehow let God be the bevel

Stand Up Tall

When you feel like you could fall
Make it a point to stand up tall
Stress can cause derangement
Then you need encouragement

Be happy for what you have
Being strong, you have the stave
Conform to life and truly see
What is not, what can be

People have fear if a problem appears
Feel unworthy to their peers
You can look up to God
He might spare the rod

Start each day as a new beginning
Soon you will be winning
Believe in yourself, God believes in you
Without a doubt, you get through

Be happy and joyous
Make life boisterous
When changes need to be made
Try not to be afraid

God knows our heart
With you he will not part
He does help you see the way
Make it worthwhile today

Take Control

Move from being the spectator
Become the speaker
Do not sit back trying to hide
Move forth and do your part with pride

Instead of being quiet, take control
Let the pattern show the toll
With your opinion, give it all
Being up to you to take the call

Instead of just asking questions
Answer within the dimensions
Take control so it's not unbearable
Control your life so it's not perishable

The need to open up and become alive
Have the quest to survive
Contribute to accomplishments
See the need for commitments

Move from inside to outside
All you need to do is abide
Take control and move from idle
Find out how to grasp your title

It is time to take control
Don't waste time and just loll
Switch position from off to on
Make yourself higher than a pawn

The Cross

I pray we remember the day of the cross
I pray we remember you were there for us
When we want things to be our way
What if Jesus wanted it his way

You have to go through the pain
Feel like you're going to drain
The need to know the suffering
It's not the end, it's the beginning

To think you're at the bottom of it all
Does not mean you will have to fall
At times it will be the last key
That fits the lock and will help you see

God, all I have is yours
All I am is yours
Jesus died for our sins
The cross reminds us of its wins

Next comes the raising up
Then you drink from your cup
Remember Jesus died for you and me
The cross has meaning to believe

The Lord Is My Protector

Lord, my protector, knows what I need
Now you are the one that must heed
Take this notice and be aware
Do not take this lightly, be not austere

From this day forward, it has been said
For all to open their eyes, make an amend
Bring up your armor, put it on
Ready to use it, you must don

Above all else, the end is near
The showings have been made clear
The days get shorter, time is important
We must be upon this, not be impotent

Walk forward, not back, take your stand
Anything needed will gladly upstand
Listen, look, and see what is to be
Draw even closer, not away from me

This I say with all my might
It is now time to get ready to fight
Take the time to put your armor on
Take the time to see the dawn

Today

Starting today is the way
To go and know what to say
Everything will be all right
Every day and every night

We watch, and we think
God is there to help us in a wink
He knows we love him, he loves us
He really does

Today starts the rest of the days
We know we do as he says
Everything is going to be fine
We are his, he says you are mine

Today is the beginning of tomorrow
Do not go forward with sorrow
Because he loves us, he is with us
Tomorrow he will be in us

Go forward and smile with all your might
Look at it with good sight
Day, night, it will be all right
Today starts tomorrow, and it is right

Today, tomorrow, and after that
We care, he cares. He is the welcome mat
So go forward from here
He is with us, he is everywhere

We Will See

We will see God's light
It will shine so bright
Giving birth to a new beginning
Then you know you are winning

Take it one step at a time if needed
As beads go on a string to get beaded
You will blossom as you grow
Just as sure as the wind will blow

Look up at the sky with sunlight
Even the stars shine at night
Relax in the beauty
With God accept your duty

Practical, knowing, and loved
You see the good, no longer odd
We will see God's light
It will shine so bright

Remember that you are never alone
We will see God's promise, and condone
We will see achievements every day
God will walk with you all the way

When God Says

When God says step away
You need to obey
When God says step back
You can see the attack

When God says be still and listen
You will hear the tension lessen
When God says move forward
It does not mean fall backward

When God says feel the pain
The burden will not remain
When God says have concentration
You begin to feel the vibration

When God says look at what can be
You notice the difference with you and me
You look past what is apparent
Then you see the transparent

When God says sing unto me
We open our mouth with glee
When God says the end will come
You prepare with armor and succumb

Working

God, work with us
We need you to help us
To learn, we need your teaching
To teach ourselves, we need your guiding

Jesus, work within us
With your help, we will learn forgiveness
We need to let go of anger
With your help, health is not in danger

Holy Spirit, work through us
Take away our pain and heal us
Help to always lift us up
You know how to pick us up

God, I ask you to protect us
Jesus, we ask to feel your love for us
Holy Spirit, your miracles sustain us
Working together, it will contain us

Working Together

Working together, we become as one
Making sure God's work gets done
Working in tune to help one another
No jealousy against one or the other

Steadily we continue our work
This is good, there is no quirk
As bees work together in a hive
We work together and not deprive

Together we unite and serve
We make it around the curve
As our work is finished
The problem is diminished

At the end, we can elate
Happiness is our trait
Work together to bring out hope
Happy together and not mope

Working together keeps us in tune
The music will start soon
Pay attention to the harmony
Working together plays the way

You Have a Father

When it hurts the most
Remember to think foremost
Life is a learning process
Not something to guess

Try to get it right the first time
Hard because it has to rhyme
Pray, love, need, want, grow
Do not let fear intrude on what you know

Everyone has problems in their lives
You can make it through the drives
Drive to places you know and have to go
Take a chance and ask God fast or slow

Things can change right before your eyes
What you thought was truth might be lies
Try to reinforce positive from negative
Have good in the way you live

With nothing, you have a Father, a home
You don't have to be lost and just roam
Ask for help and you will receive
From your heart, you must believe

Arlene truly shows her love for the Lord and her faith in him as she writes her poems. I value her as a person and treasure my friendship with her and dearly love her.

—Patsy O'Neal

Arlene is a loving woman and filled with faith. I have known her from grade school, and to me she is a sister. Poetry is her therapy from problems. Her poems are sure to lift your heart and your faith.

—Cathie Kerekes

This is a very special kind of book, and I think it deserves a few words to accompany it on its journey out into the hands of those that will find enjoyment while reading this book of poetry. All the poems in this book are birthed from the heart of God and are about life itself. I have had the privilege of reading some of the poems written by Arlene, and I believe that as you read these poems, you will find yourself in a journey that many people happen to find themselves on. As you find yourself on this journey, you will be able to know you are not alone. I encourage you to acquire the joy from reading these poems.

—Pastor Dale Cornell